Play MORMON HYMNS

16 Piano Arrangements of Traditional Hymns

Arranged by **Linda Christensen**
and **David M. Love**

Dorsey Music
1231 Caldwell Blvd.
Nampa, ID 83651

In the *Play MORMON HYMNS* series, pianists young and old will find accessible arrangements of beloved hymns, which are a continuous source of inspiration and an important part of worship services. These selections have been carefully chosen to include hymns of praise, supplication, and the Restoration.

It is best for piano students to observe the rhythms as notated, but these may be adjusted later to match what they have heard at worship services.

The joy found in learning these arrangements will result in performers who love to *Play MORMON HYMNS.*

Alfred Music
P.O. Box 10003
Van Nuys, CA 91410-0003
alfred.com

Copyright © 2017 by Alfred Music
All rights reserved. Printed in USA.

ISBN-10: 1-4706-3959-9
ISBN-13: 978-1-4706-3959-4

Cover Art: Golden Angel Moroni Atop Timpanogos Temple: © Getty Images / kenhl • Temple in San Diego: © Getty Images / photoquest7

Abide with Me!

Words by Henry F. Lyte
Music by William H. Monk
Arr. David M. Love

When oth - er help - ers fail and com - forts flee,

Help of the help - less, oh, a - bide with me!

Battle Hymn of the Republic

Words by Julia Ward Howe
Traditional Folk Song
Arr. David M. Love

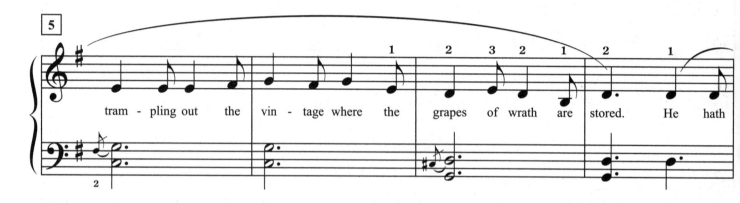

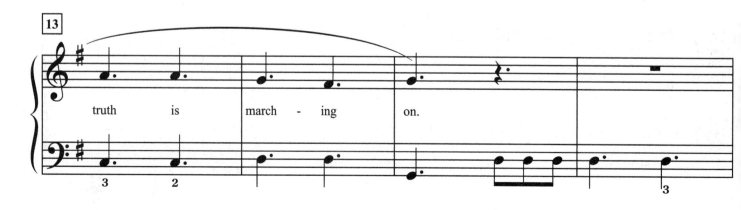

Come, Listen to a Prophet's Voice

Words by Joseph S. Murdock
Music by Joseph J. Daynes
Arr. Linda Christensen

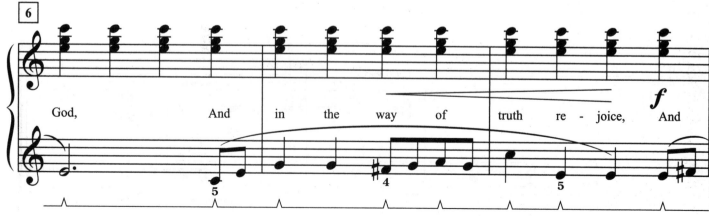

Did You Think to Pray?

Words by Mary A. Pepper Kidder
Music by William O. Perkins
Arr. Linda Christensen

9

Have I Done Any Good?

Words and Music by Will L. Thompson
Arr. David M. Love

How Great the Wisdom and the Love

Words by Eliza R. Snow
Music by Thomas McIntyre
Arr. Linda Christensen

I Stand All Amazed

Words and Music by Charles H. Gabriel
Arr. Linda Christensen

Jesus, the Very Thought of Thee

Words Attr. to Bernard of Clairvaux
Music by John B. Dykes
Arr. David M. Love

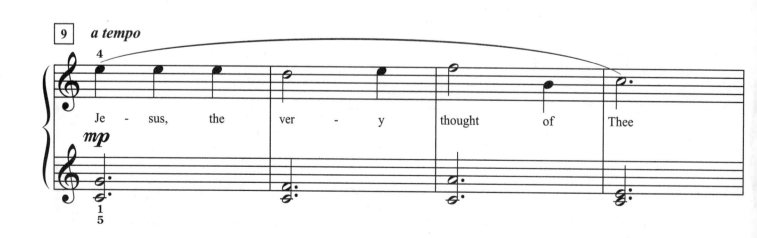

Je - sus, the ver - y thought of Thee

Joseph Smith's First Prayer

Words by George Manwaring
Music by Sylvanus Billings Pond
Arr. David M. Love

in the shad - y wood - land Jo - seph sought the God of

Slower

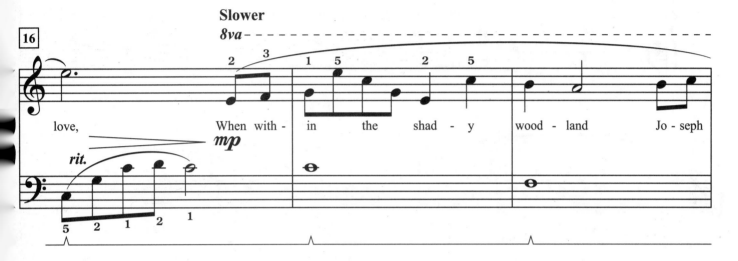

love, When with - in the shad - y wood - land Jo - seph

Tempo I

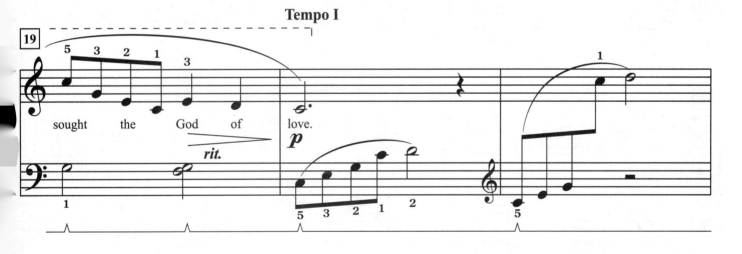

sought the God of love.

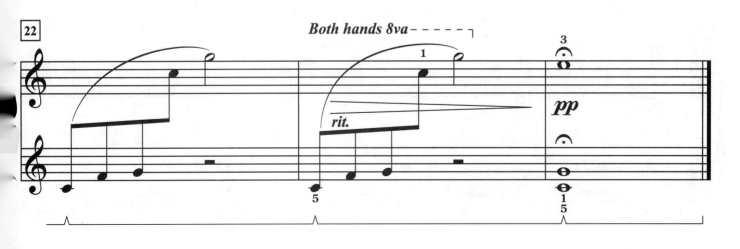

Let Us Oft Speak Kind Words

Words by Joseph L. Townsend
Music by Ebenezer Beesley
Arr. Linda Christensen

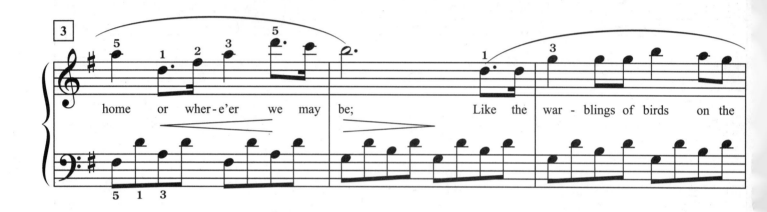

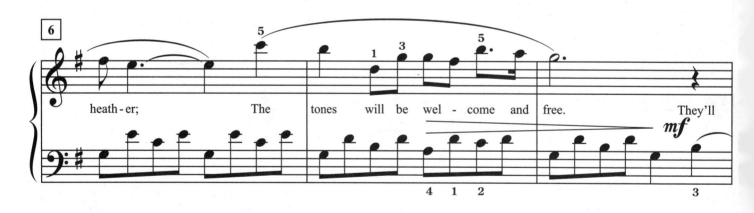

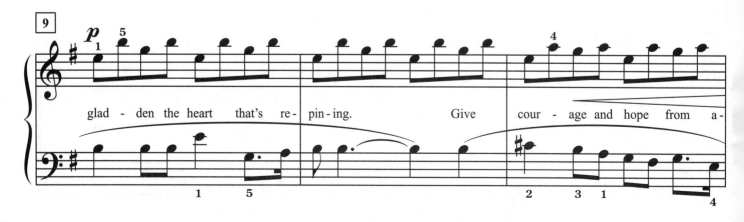

More Holiness Give Me

Words and Music by Philip Paul Bliss
Arr. Linda Christensen

O My Father

Words by Eliza R. Snow
Music by James McGranahan
Arr. Linda Christensen

hol - ly hab - i - ta - tion, Did my spir - it once re -

side? In my first pri - me - val child - hood Was I

nur - tured near Thy side?

Praise to the Lord, the Almighty

Words by Joachim Neander
Stralsund Gesangbuch
Arr. David M. Love

Praise to the Man

Words by William W. Phelps
Scottish Folk Song
Arr. David M. Love

Hail to the Proph - et, as - cend - ed to heav - en! Trai - tors and ty - rants now

fight him in vain. Min - gling with Gods, he can plan for his breth - ren;

Death can - not con - quer the he - ro a - gain.

We Thank Thee, O God, for a Prophet

Words by William Fowler
Music by Caroline Sheridan Norton
Arr. Linda Christensen

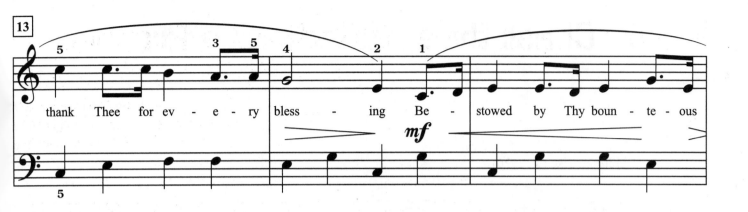

thank Thee for ev - e - ry bless - ing Be - stowed by Thy boun - te - ous

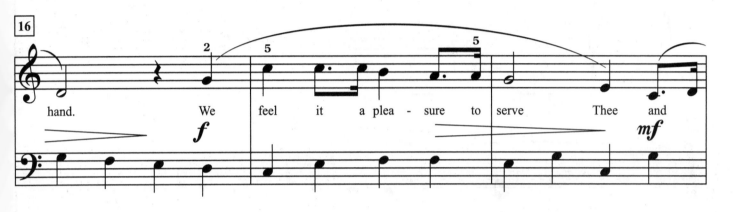

hand. We feel it a plea - sure to serve Thee and

love to o - bey Thy com - mand.

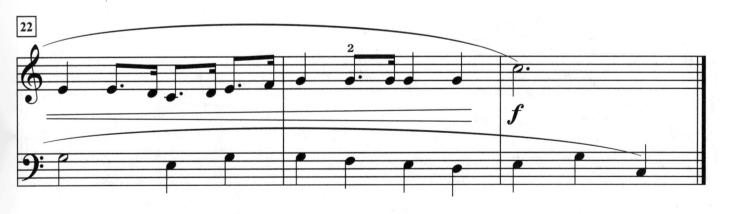

Christ the Lord Is Risen Today

Words by Charles Wesley
Lyra Davidica
Arr. David M. Love